Visual C++® 2008
Programming Companion

Visual C++® 2008
Programming Companion

Andrés Becerra

Boston　San Francisco　New York
London　Toronto　Sydney　Tokyo　Singapore　Madrid
Mexico City　Munich　Paris　Cape Town　Hong Kong　Montreal

Executive Editor:	Michael Hirsch
Acquisitions Editor:	Matt Goldstein
Editorial Assistant:	Sarah Milmore
Senior Production Supervisor:	Marilyn Lloyd
Compositor and Cover Designer:	Laura Wiegleb
Marketing Manager:	Christopher Kelly
Senior Manufacturing Buyer:	Carol Melville
Media Buyer:	Ginny Michaud

Many of the designations used by manufacturers and sellers to distinguish their products are claimed as trademarks. Where those designations appear in this book, and Addison-Wesley was aware of a trademark claim, the designations have been printed in initial caps or all caps.

Microsoft® Visual C++ development system copyright © Microsoft Corporation. 1985–2008. All rights reserved.

The programs and applications presented in this book have been included for their instructional value. They have been tested with care but are not guaranteed for any particular purpose. Neither the publisher nor the author offers any warranties or representations, nor do they accept any liabilities with respect to the program or applications.

Dedicated to Becki and Sito.

Copyright © 2009 Pearson Education, Inc. All rights reserved. No part of this publication may be reproduced, stored in a retrieval system, or transmitted, in any form or by any means, electronic, mechanical, photocopying, recording, or otherwise, without the prior written permission of the publisher. Printed in the United States of America. For information on obtaining permission for use of material in this work, please submit a written request to Pearson Education, Inc., Rights and Contracts Department, 501 Boylston Street, Suite 900, Boston, MA 02116, fax your request to 617-671-3447, or e-mail at http://www.pearsoned.com/legal/permissions.htm.

ISBN 0-321-54112-X

1 2 3 4 5 6 7 8 9 10—CRS—11 10 09 08

Contents

Introduction   1

Introduction to Windows   1
What is Windows?   1
Navigating the Windows Environment   1
Applications   5

Visual C++ 2008 Express Edition   5
Overview   5
Installing the Software   5
Visual C++ 2008 Express Edition IDE   11
Creating Your First Program   13
Saving Projects   18
Opening Existing Projects   19

Debugging Projects   20
What is Debugging?   20
Debugging Techniques   20
Visual C++ 2008 Express Edition Debugging Features   20

Graphical User Interface (GUI) Applications   27
Overview   27
Recreating the Console Program as a GUI   27
Week Number Finder GUI Project   29

Index   34

Introduction

This book introduces the beginner programmer to the Microsoft Windows operating system and Microsoft Visual C++ 2008® Express Edition development environment. This book will explain fundamentals about navigating in the Windows operating system as well as the Visual C++ 2008 Express Edition Integrated Development Environment (IDE).

Visual C++ 2008 can be used to create simple text-based console applications as well as windows-based graphical user applications (GUI). This book will guide the beginner programmer through the process of downloading and installing the Visual C++ 2008 Express Edition software on a computer, using the Visual C++ 2008 Express Edition IDE, and creating sample applications while applying debugging techniques.

The sample applications that you will create in this guide can also be downloaded from my website, along with additional code samples not documented in this guide, http://AndresBecerra.com/ProgrammingCompanion/

Introduction to Windows

What is Windows?

Windows is an operating system that is written by Microsoft Corporation. Operating systems are special programs that control how a computer runs and allow other programs to run. Windows provides a graphical environment for navigating among various elements of your computer. In order to learn how to create your own programs, you must first be familiar with how to work with the Windows operating system. Microsoft provides different versions of the Windows operating system such as Windows 98, Windows 2000 and Windows XP. This book will use pictures of the Windows XP operating system, but will note important differences for the Windows 2000 operating system as appropriate.

Navigating the Windows Environment

Logging In to Windows

The first step to using the Windows operating system is to log in to the computer. Most Windows XP computers are configured to start with a simplified login screen, where you can choose from a list of user names to log in with (see Figure 1). A system administrator may choose to configure your computer so a more traditional

FIGURE 1 Windows XP New Style Login

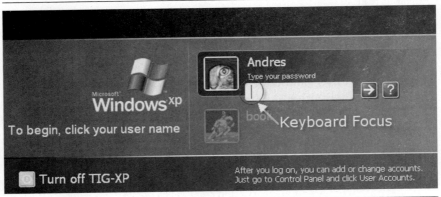

login screen is presented (see Figure 2). This traditional login screen is very similar to the login screen you will see if you are using Windows 2000, and you will have to press the *Ctrl+Alt+Del* keys on the keyboard at the same time to see it. In either case, make sure the keyboard focus (noted by a vertical line) is in the correct field by clicking that field with your mouse. Type in your user name and password and then hit the *Enter* key.

Desktop Overview

Once you are logged in to the Windows operating system, you will be presented with the *Windows Desktop* (see Figure 3). The Windows Desktop is comprised of a number of components. The long gray bar at the bottom of the screen contains the *Start Button*, the *Task Bar* and the *System Tray*. The *Start Button* is used to access all

FIGURE 2 Windows XP Traditional Style Login

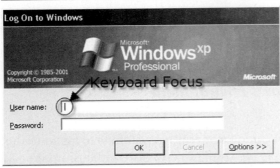

FIGURE 3 Windows Desktop

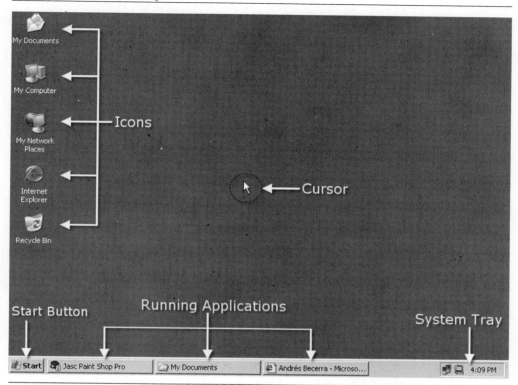

the installed applications on your computer. The *Task Bar* shows what applications are currently running. The *System Tray* shows commonly used applications that are always running as well as the current time. The desktop also contains *icons* that are shortcuts to commonly used applications. In the middle of the screen is a small arrow called the *cursor*. You can move the cursor around the screen using your mouse. Quickly clicking on an icon twice (double-clicking the icon) will open the application with which that icon is associated.

Exploring Files and Folders

On the desktop, double-click the *My Computer* icon. If you are using a Windows XP computer, you will probably see a window similar to the screen shown in Figure 4. If you are using a Windows 2000 computer or your system administrator has configured Windows XP to look like Windows 2000, you will see a window similar to the screen shown in Figure 5.

FIGURE 4 Windows XP My Computer

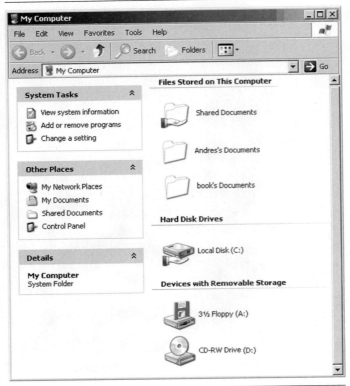

FIGURE 5 Windows 2000 My Computer

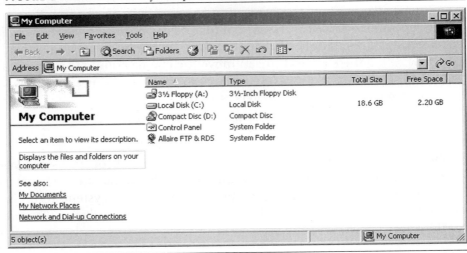

In either case, you will see a summary of folders and drives available on your computer. At least one of the items will be labeled *Local Disk (C:)*. This item is your hard drive, where all operating system (i.e. Windows 2000 or Windows XP) and important system files are stored. This is also the same hard drive where you will probably save the application files you write while following this guide.

Another item you will see is *3½ Floppy (A:)*, which is your removable floppy disk drive. Students sometimes use this drive to save their project files in class, and then take the floppy disk home with them to continue working on their project from home.

Applications

Applications are tools built by a programmer that allow a computer user to perform a specific task on a computer. A few examples of applications are an Internet web browser, an email software package or a painting program to draw pictures. Applications are also referred to as programs.

Although there are many applications already built and available to computer users, there is always a need for existing applications to be maintained or entirely new applications to be written from scratch. One of the main roles a programmer fills is to build and maintain applications. This guide is designed to help you get started with creating your own applications in the Visual C++ 2008 Express Edition programming environment.

Visual C++ 2008 Express Edition

Overview

Visual C++ 2008 Express Edition is a software package that needs to be installed on your computer before you can begin writing C++ applications. The entire installation process will take between 20 minutes and 3 hours, depending on the speed and configuration of your computer and internet connection. It is an easy install even for novices. The instructions in the next section will guide you through each step. If you have any difficulty, you should talk to your instructor.

Installing the Software

1. The software can be downloaded from Microsoft's website. Open your Internet Explorer (IE) web browser, click your mouse in the "Address" field, and type the following in:

    http://www.microsoft.com/express/download/

    After a few seconds, you should see the web page shown in Figure 6.

FIGURE 6 Visual C++ 2008 Express Edition Download Web Page

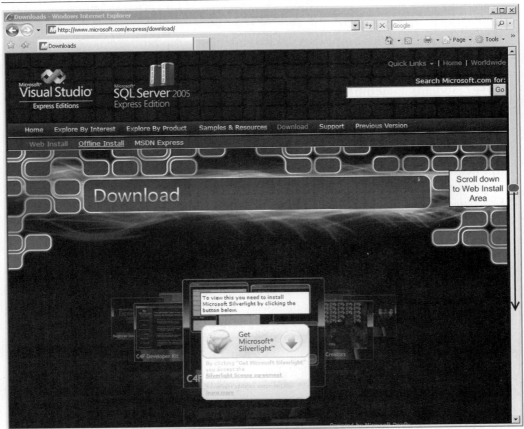

2. You might see a notice (shown in Figure 6) prompting you to Get Microsoft Silverlight. If so, just ignore it and scroll further down the web page until you reach the Web Install section. In the Visual C++ 2008 box (bottom right), choose "English" from the dropdown list (Figure 7, #1). You might receive an IE security prompt (Figure 7, #2). If so, right-click the security prompt bar and then choose Download File (Figure 7, #3).

3. At this point IE will prompt you to run or save the setup program. Click the Run button as shown in Figure 8. Once the download has completed, the Setup program will begin to run and IE will again prompt you to run or save the secondary setup program. Click the Run button as shown in Figure 9.

FIGURE 7 Web Install

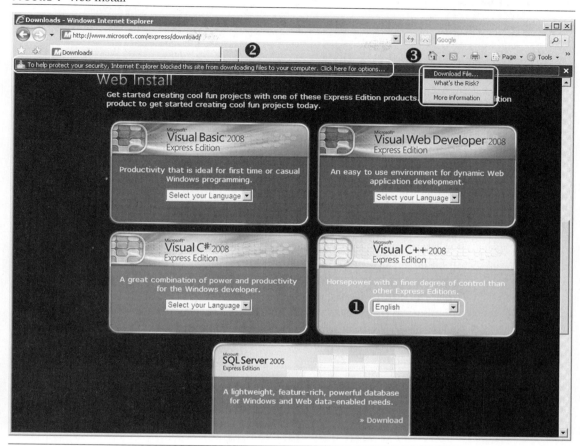

FIGURE 8 File Download

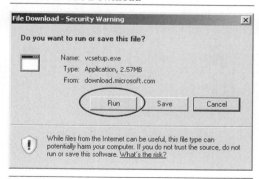

FIGURE 9 Downloading

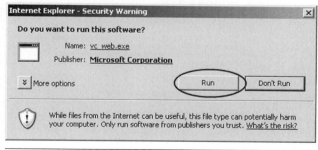

FIGURE 10 Setup Loading

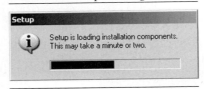

4. After the *Setup* loading screen completes (Figure 10), the Micorosft Visual C++ 2008 Express Edition Setup window will appear on the "Welcome to Setup" step. Simply click the Next button to proceed with installation of Visual C++ 2008.

5. Next is the *License Terms* step (Figure 11). Read the Microsoft Software License Terms, choose the "I have read and accept the license terms" option, then click the Next button.

6. On the *Installation Options* step, you will be able to choose different installation options as shown in Figure 12. While both the MSDN Express Library for Visual Studio 2008 and Microsoft Silverlight Runtime are optional components, it is highly recommended that you choose these installation options as well. The MSDN Library provides you with a treasure trove of documentation and code samples at your finger tips.

FIGURE 11 License Terms

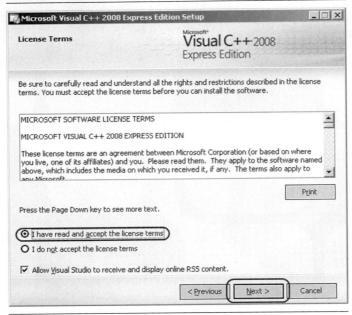

Visual C++ 2008 Express Edition 9

FIGURE 12 Installation Options

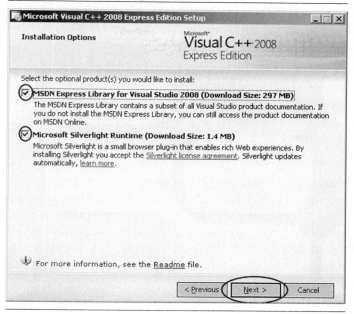

FIGURE 13 Destination Folder

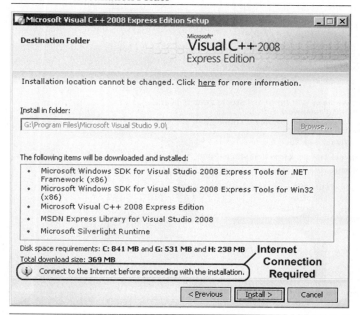

7. The next screen will be the *Destination Folder*, shown in Figure 13. It is important to note that an **Internet Connection is Required**. A broadband internet connection is highly recommended for installing Visual C++ 2008 Express Edition.

   By default, Visual C++ 2008 Express Edition will be installed on your C:\ drive. If you do not have enough room on your C:\ drive, click the *Browse*...button to choose another hard drive. If you don't have another hard drive, you will have to try and remove some files on your C:\ drive to free up more space.

   When you are ready, click the *Install >* button.

8. The *Download and Install Progress* window is where a bulk of your installation time will be spent (see Figure 14). The setup program has to first download necessary files, before it will actually start to install the files. Once downloading has completed, the screen will update showing you which files are being installed (Figure 15) and their installation progress. Note that you can disconnect from the internet, if you need to, once all files have been downloaded.

FIGURE 14 Download Progress

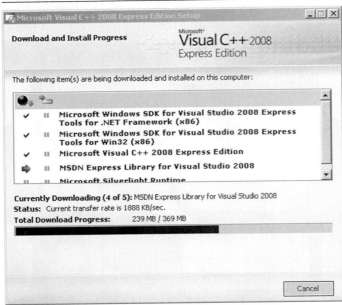

9. Once the download and install steps have completed, you will be presented with a *Setup Complete* screen as shown in Figure 16.

   At some point, it would be a good idea to register the product with Microsoft. At this moment, however, it is not essential. For now, just click the *Exit* button.

Visual C++ 2008 Express Edition IDE

Now that you have Visual C++ 2008 Express Edition installed, let's take a look at the Integrated Development Environment (IDE). To start Visual C++ 2008 Express Edition, click the Start button, then *All Programs* (Programs in Windows 2000), then *Visual C++ 9.0 Express Edition* and then the *Microsoft Visual C++ 2008 Express Edition* icon.

FIGURE 15 Installation Progress

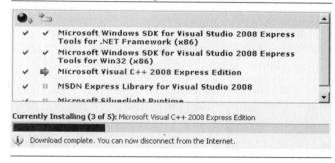

FIGURE 16 Setup Complete

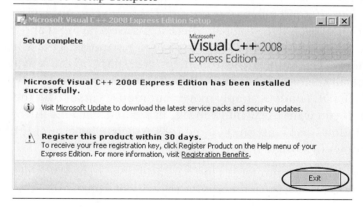

FIGURE 17 Visual C++ 2008 Express Edition Integrated Development Environment

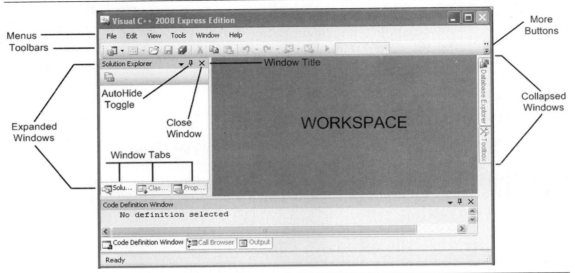

The Visual C++ 2008 Express Edition IDE has many different "pieces" to it. The major pieces are described below and highlighted in Figure 17:

- **Workspace**—The workspace is the main window in the IDE. This is where you will spend the most time writing programming code and designing your own windows.

- **IDE Windows**—Most windows within the IDE are dockable. This means the window edges can "stick" to the outer edges of the Workspace area of the IDE. To move a dockable window, click and hold the left mouse button on the *Window Title* and move your mouse. There are also two icons in the top-right corner of each IDE Window. These icons are a pushpin and an "X". The pushpin toggles the *AutoHide* feature of an IDE Window. The "X" *closes* the IDE Window. The AutoHide feature helps save space on the screen by automatically collapsing (or hiding) the IDE Window when not in use. To expand the IDE Window, simply move your mouse cursor over the collapsed window. If you want the window to stay expanded, click the pushpin icon. Some Windows also contain *Window Tabs*, which allow grouping of multiple IDE windows in a single IDE Window.

- **Toolbars**—There are numerous toolbars available in the IDE. All toolbars are merely shortcuts for actions you can perform from the menus. If the toolbar contains more buttons that can be viewed on screen at once, then a special icon is shown at the end of the toolbar. This icon allows you to view *more buttons* on the toolbar. You can also reposition toolbars in the IDE by clicking and holding the left mouse button on the left side of the toolbar, then moving the mouse within the IDE.

- **Menus**—The menu is always available in the IDE and provides every action you can take within the IDE. Toolbars are merely shortcuts to clicking through menu entries. If you accidentally close a window, you can use the *View* menu to re-open the window.

Creating Your First Program

When you open the Visual C++ 2008 Express Edition IDE, you are typically greeted with the *Start Page* in the workspace area (Figure 18).

The *Recent Projects* area provides a list of existing projects you have worked on recently. Projects help you organize all the files that comprise a Visual C++ 2008 Express Edition program you create. The first time you run the software, this list will be empty. Click the *Project...* link next to *Create:* to create a new C++ project. The *New Project* screen allows you to specify many different options for the new project (see Figure 19). There are several *project templates* for each of the *project types*. The first application we create will be a Win32 Console project by following these steps:

1. Choose *Win32* under *Project Types*.
2. Choose *Win32 Console Application* under *Templates*.

FIGURE 18 C++.Net Start Page

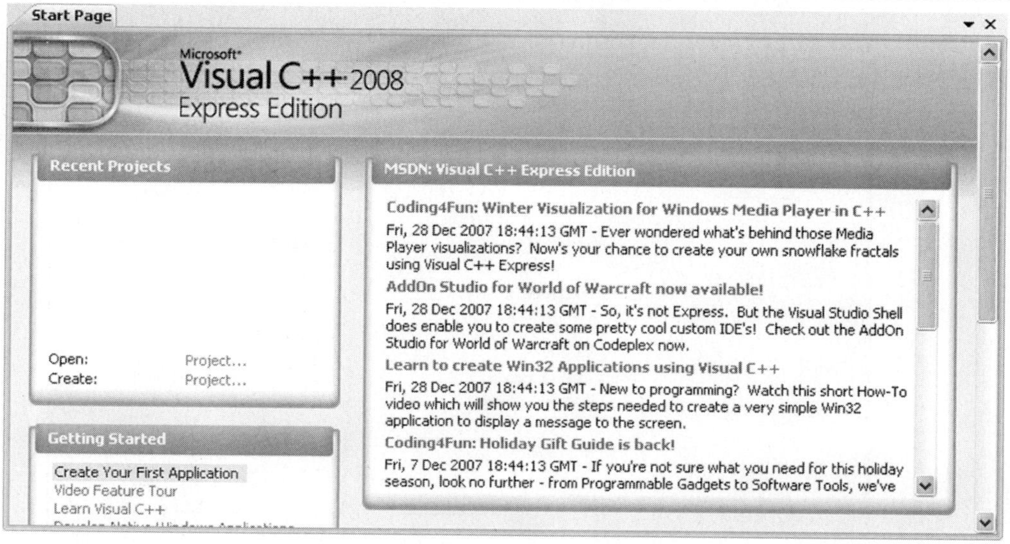

FIGURE 19 Create a New Win32 Console Project

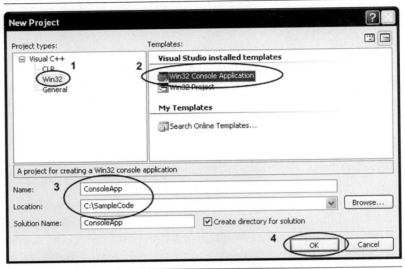

3. Provide a name for the project in the *Name* text field.
4. Click the *OK* button.

The *Win32 Application Wizard* will help you get started in creating your first C++ application. In order to continue, click *Application Settings* and make sure the *Application Type* is set to *Console Application* and *Precompiled header* is checked before clicking the *Finish* button (as shown in Figure 20).

FIGURE 20 Win32 Application Wizard

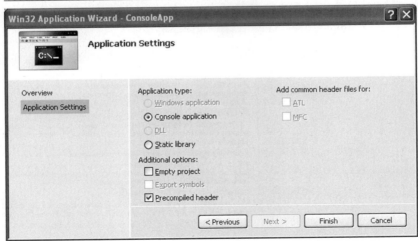

FIGURE 21 Win32 Console App - Skeleton Program

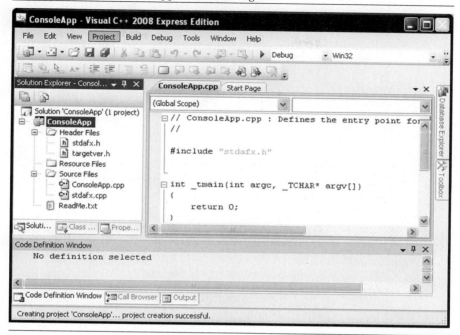

The *Win32 Application Wizard* creates a skeleton program to help you get started. At this point, the IDE will show items in the *Solution Explorer* as well as an open file called *ConsoleApp.cpp* in the *Workspace* (see Figure 21). The open file is ConsoleApp.cpp, the main source code file of your application. There will also be a few new windows at the bottom of the IDE. The only one of importance right now is the *Output Window*.

Customizing the Skeleton Program

Now you can start customizing the skeleton program by typing in your own source code. In order to keep things easy, you will create a simple Fahrenheit to Celsius degree conversion application. You can start by clicking within the ConsoleApp.cpp code window then typing in the code below. When you are finished, the code window should look something like Figure 22.

```
#include "stdafx.h"
#include "conio.h"
#include <iostream>
using namespace std;

int _tmain(int argc, _TCHAR* argv[])
{
    double fahrenheit;
    double celsius;

    //Get the temperature in fahrenheit
    cout<<"Enter the temperature in fahrenheit: ";
    cin>>fahrenheit;

    //Convert the temperature to celsius
    celsius = (fahrenheit-32)/1.8;

    //Display the temperature in celsius
    cout<<"The temperature in celsius is "<<celsius<<endl;

    //Pause so user can see the result
    printf("Press any key to continue");
    char n = _getch();
    return 0;
}
```

Building the Program

The process of building a program involves the Visual C++ 2008 Express Edition IDE parsing and compiling your source code. To build a program, click the *Build* menu, and then click *Build Solution* (or hit the *F7* key). Messages will be displayed in the *Output Window* while your program is being built. If there are no errors in your program, the *Output Window* will have the following message:

```
==== Build: 1 succeeded, 0 failed, 0 up-to-date, 0 skipped ====
```

If there are any errors in your program, they will show in the *Output Window*. Check the *Output Window*, fix any errors that are shown, and then build the program again.

FIGURE 22 Win32 Console App - Completed Code

```cpp
//ConsoleApp.cpp: Defines the entry point for the //console application.
#include "stdafx.h"
#include "conio.h"
#include <iostream>
using namespace std;

int _tmain(int argc, _TCHAR* argv[])
{
    double fahrenheit;
    double celsius;

    //Get the temperature in fahrenheit
    cout<<"Enter the temperature in fahrenheit: ";
    cin>>fahrenheit;

    //Convert the temperature to celsius
    celsius = (fahrenheit-32)/1.8;

    //Display the temperature in celsius
    cout<<"The temperature in celsius is "<<celsius<<endl;

    //Pause so user can see the result
    printf("Press any key to continue");
    char n = getch();
    return 0;
}
```

Running the Program

You can run and test your program after a successful build using one of two options: run with debugging and run without debugging. If you run with debugging, you will be able to type in a Fahrenheit value and hit the Enter key, but the conversion result will quickly flash by and the console application window will close before you get a chance to see the result. Running a program with debugging is useful when you want to step through code (more on that later). For this first sample, let's run the application without debugging. To do this, click the *Debug* menu, and then click *Start Without Debugging* or use the keyboard shortcut Ctrl+F5 (see Figure 23).

FIGURE 23 Debug Menu

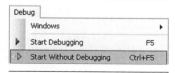

A separate window will open that will prompt you for input. This is actually the program you just made! Test the application by typing in a numeric value for Fahrenheit degrees, then hit the Enter key. The program should do the Fahrenheit to Celsius conversion, display it in the console application window and then wait for you to press any key to continue (as shown in Figure 24). Press a key to close the console application window and return to the Visual C++ 2008 Express Edition IDE.

Saving Projects

Save Early, Save Often
— Sierra regarding their King's Quest video game series.

Saving your work is a very important task. You should get into the habit of doing it often. You never know when something unexpected could happen such as a power failure or someone tripping over the power cord to your computer. If you have spent hours typing in code without saving, you can potentially lose all that hard work.

The quickest and easiest way to save your work is by clicking the *File* menu, and then clicking *Save All* (see Figure 25). You can also click the *Save All* icon on the toolbar.

After saving your project, you can safely exit the Visual C++ 2008 Express Edition IDE by clicking the *File* menu, and then clicking *Exit*.

Opening Existing Projects

The most convenient way to open an existing project is to use the *Start Page* within the Visual C++ 2008 Express Edition IDE. This page shows projects that were worked on recently (see Figure 26). Click the name of the project (in this case ConsoleApp) to open the existing project. If you want to open a different project, you can click the *Open Project* button and browse to the project file on the hard drive or floppy disk.

FIGURE 24 Win32 Console Application

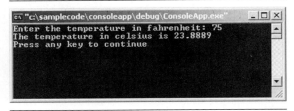

FIGURE 25 File Menu

FIGURE 26 Opening an Existing Project

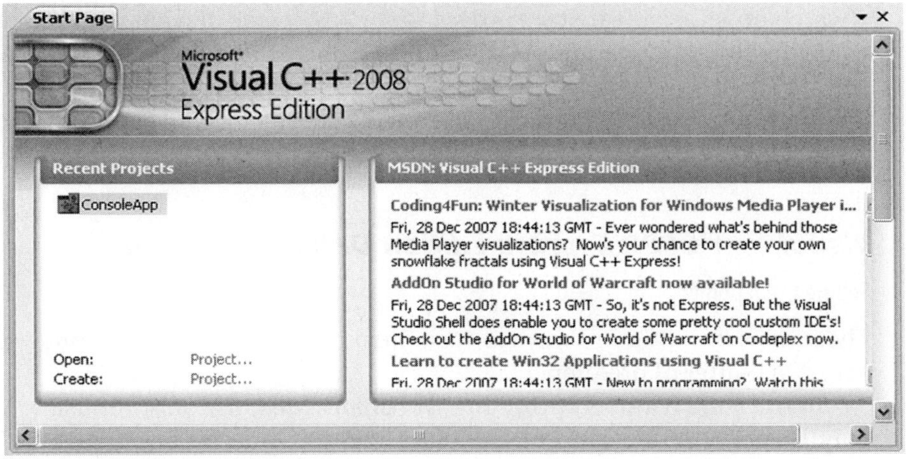

Debugging Projects

What is Debugging?

Debugging is the process of finding errors (also known as bugs) in a program and fixing them. Sometimes an error is easy to find; other times an error is notoriously difficult to track down. The Visual C++ 2008 Express Edition IDE provides many features to help make the debugging process easier and more efficient.

Debugging Techniques

Breakpoints

A breakpoint is a visual indicator you can place in the IDE to make a program pause on a certain line. Breakpoints are typically used in conjunction with stepping through code.

Stepping Through Code

The lines of code in a program normally run at a speed too fast for the human eye to follow. Stepping through code allows a programmer to execute one line at a time at his or her own pace.

Watching Variables

A watch on a variable helps a programmer keep track of what is stored in a variable while the program is running. Creating a watch is typically used when a variable is getting set to an invalid value, but the programmer does not know where the value is getting set. A watch helps a programmer identify in what situation a variable gets set to an invalid value.

Visual C++ 2008 Express Edition Debugging Features

Setting Breakpoints

There are a few different ways to set a breakpoint in code. Which one you choose is simply a matter of preference.

In the code window within the *Workspace area*, use your mouse to click on the gray bar on the left side of the code window on the line you wish to set the breakpoint. A red dot will appear as well as a momentary message showing where the breakpoint was set (as shown in Figure 27).

In the code window within the *Workspace area*, right-click with your mouse on the line of code you wish to set the break point. When the popup menu appears, click *Insert Breakpoint* (as shown in Figure 28) and the red dot will appear on that line showing that the breakpoint was set.

Let's try setting a breakpoint and watching how the IDE stops at the breakpoint. Set a breakpoint on the following line of code as shown in Figure 29:

```
celsius = (fahrenheit-32)/1.8;
```

When you are ready, click the *Debug* menu, and then click *Start* (or just hit the F5 key). The program will start running and will pause once it reaches the breakpoint.

FIGURE 27 Setting a Breakpoint #1

```
        double fahrenheit;
        double celsius;

        //Get the temperature in fahrenheit
        cout<<"Enter the temperature in fahrenheit: ";
        cin>>fahrenheit;
At ConsoleApp.cpp, line 14 ('_tmain(int argc, _TCHAR* argv[])', line 7)
        //Convert the temperature to celsius
        celsius = (fahrenheit-32)/1.8;

        //Display the temperature in celsius
        cout<<"The temperature in celsius is "<<celsius<<endl;
```

FIGURE 28 Setting a Breakpoint #2

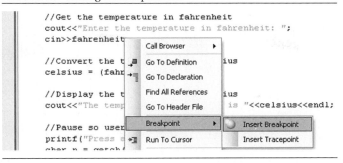

You will see a yellow arrow within the red dot that symbolizes the breakpoint (see Figure 30). This yellow arrow shows the next line of code that will be executed. At this point you have many options on what to do next. You can "peek" at the value of a variable by holding your mouse over the variable (also shown in Figure 30). You can step through the remainder of the code (more on stepping in a bit). You can also choose to simply continue running the program by hitting the F5 key.

FIGURE 29 ConsoleApp Breakpoint

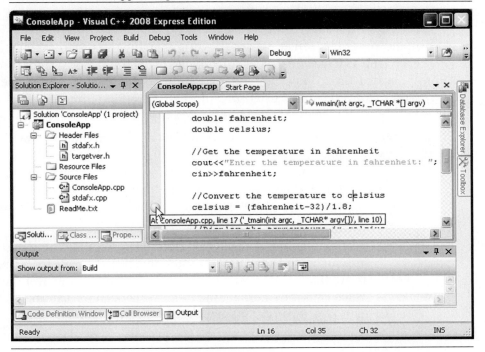

FIGURE 30 Current Line of Execution

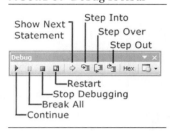

FIGURE 31 Debug Toolbar

While the program is running, the *Debug Toolbar* becomes available as a shortcut to the *Debug* menu options (see Figure 31). If your program is currently at a breakpoint, you can use the *Debug Toolbar* to *continue* running the program, *stop debugging* the program or *restart* the program. If you scrolled the code window to another portion of the code sample and forgot which statement will be the next to execute, use the *show next statement* option on the *Debug Toolbar*. This will automatically scroll the code window so the next line of code to execute comes into view. There are also the *Step Into*, *Step Over*, and *Step Out* options on the *Debug Toolbar* which we will discuss next.

Step Into, Over and Out

Normally, programs run at full speed without giving the programmer a chance to see each step as it executes. A useful debugging technique is to step through code one line at a time. You can start stepping through a program once it hits a breakpoint, or you can start stepping through a program from the very first line of code. There are three different stepping modes: step into, step over and step out.

- **Step Into**—This is the most detailed form of code stepping, allowing you to view each line of code as it executes. If the current line of code calls an external function, then the IDE will step into that external function and continue stepping through the code line-by-line in the function. When the function completes, the IDE will return to the line that called the function, and continue stepping from there.

- **Step Over**—Sometimes you will be interested in stepping through some code, without having any interest in stepping into the code for an external function. In that scenario, stepping over allows you to step over the line of code, which calls the external function. The code in the external function is still executed, but you do not have to step through it line-by-line.

- **Step Out**—If you find yourself stepping through code in a function (either intentionally or unintentionally), you do not have to step through each line of code. You can choose to step out of the function and continue stepping at the line of code that originally called the function.

Although you can use the *Debug Menu* or *Debug Toolbar* to step through code, the most convenient way is to use the keyboard shortcuts. To learn what the keyboard shortcuts are, look at *Debug Menu*. The keyboard shortcuts are noted to the right of corresponding menu entries (see Figure 32). The keyboard shortcut for *Step Into* is F11, for *Step Over* it is F10, and for *Step Out* it is Shift+F11.

Code Stepping Exercise

To get practice and a good understanding of how to code step using the *Step In*, *Step Over*, and *Step Out* techniques, follow these steps.

1. Open the ConsoleApp project you created.
2. If you haven't already done so, set a breakpoint on the following line of code:

```
celsius = (fahrenheit-32)/1.8;
```

3. Hit F11 once to start stepping through your code. This should put the yellow arrow at the beginning of the program (see Figure 33).
4. Hit F11 once again to step into the next line of code, which should be the first `cout` statement.

FIGURE 32 Debug Menu

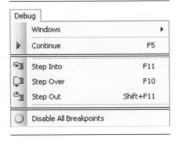

FIGURE 33 Start of Program Stepping

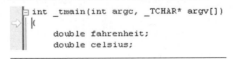

5. Hit F11 one more time and a new "ostream" code window will be opened (see Figure 34). Do not be alarmed if you don't understand the code. The code you see there is the code behind the `cout` statement. By pressing F11 (Step Into), you stepped into the code that provides the functionality for `cout`.

6. You can, of course, continue stepping through the underlying code for `cout`, but a much more convenient thing to do is to hit Shift+F11 to step out of the underlying `cout` logic.

7. Now, instead of hitting F11, hit F10 to use the Step Over technique. This should move you to the next line of code, which is the `cin` statement.

8. `cin` is similar to `cout`, in that there is underlying code that provides the `cin` functionality. If you were to hit the F11 key again, it would step into the code for `cin`. Instead of F11, use F10 to step over the `cin` line. Notice that the line still executes.

9. Hit F5 to continue running the program to the end.

FIGURE 34 Ostream Code Window

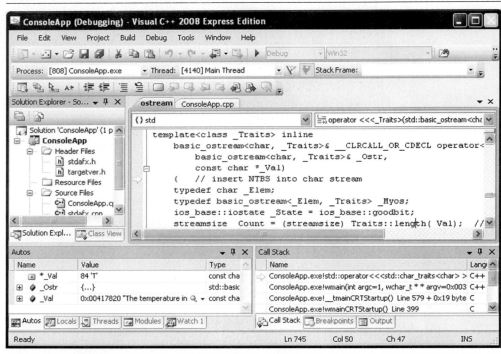

Setting Next Execution Step

As you are stepping through code, a yellow arrow will appear on the left side of the code window to show the next line of code to be executed (see Figure 33). You can use this yellow arrow to manually set the next execution step. This can come in handy if you want to re-run a section of code without having to start the program from the beginning again.

To get practice using this technique, follow these steps:

1. Set a new breakpoint in the code on the final `cout` line, which outputs the converted temperature (see Figure 35).

2. Hit F5 to run your program. The console window will open and you will be prompted to enter a Fahrenheit temperature value. Type in 80 for the value and hit the Enter key.

3. Your program should encounter the breakpoint you set in step #1. When it does, hover your mouse over the Celsius variable in the code window. Notice that the conversion from 80º Fahrenheit to ~26.6º Celsius was done (see Figure 36).

4. Click and hold the left mouse button on the yellow arrow in the code window. Without letting go of the mouse button, drag the yellow arrow to the first `cout` line where the code prompts for a Fahrenheit value (see Figure 37).

5. Hit F5 to continue and when the console window opens again notice that the prompt for Fahrenheit appears a second time (see Figure 38). Type in 70 for the value and hit the Enter key.

6. Your program should once again encounter the breakpoint you set in step #1. When it does, hold your mouse over the Celsius variable in the code

FIGURE 35 New Breakpoint

```
//Display the temperature in celsius
cout<<"The temperature in celsius is "<<celsius<<endl;
```

FIGURE 36 Pop-up Message Showing Variable Value

FIGURE 37 Setting the Next Statement

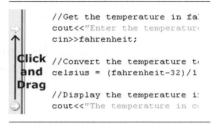

FIGURE 38 Second Prompt for Temperature

window. Notice that the value of the variable now reflects the conversion from 70º Fahrenheit to ~21.1º Celsius has taken place.

7. Hit F5 to allow the program to run to completion.

Quick Watch

A **watch** is a feature of the Visual C++ 2008 Express Edition IDE that allows you to easily track variables as a program executes. Watches can be created using a variety of techniques. A Quick Watch is the quickest and easiest way to create a watch (hence the name "Quick Watch").

To set a Quick Watch on a variable, follow these steps:

1. Hit F11 to start stepping into the code.

2. When the first line of code is marked with the yellow arrow, right click on the **celsius** variable, then click *QuickWatch*.

3. On the *QuickWatch* dialog window (see Figure 39), click the *Add Watch* button. Do not be alarmed if the *Current Value* shows "CXX0069: Error: variables need stack frame". This message is simply noting that you have not yet stepped to the line that declares the **celsius** variable. Click the *Close* button on the *QuickWatch* window.

FIGURE 39 QuickWatch Dialog Window

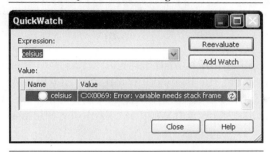

4. Continue stepping through your code and notice how the value of the variable changes within the *Watch 1* window at the bottom of the IDE (see Figure 40).
5. Hit F5 to allow the program to run to completion.

FIGURE 40 IDE with Watch 1 Window

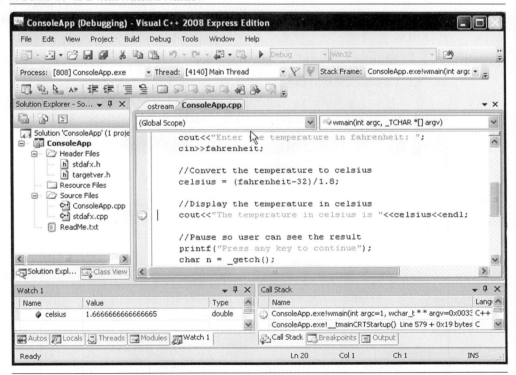

Graphical User Interface (GUI) Applications

Overview

A Graphical User Interface application is also referred to as a GUI application (pronounced gooey). A GUI provides the more common type of windows interface where users visually interact with fields and buttons on a window. Common examples of GUIs are programs like Microsoft Windows Explorer, Microsoft Internet Explorer and Microsoft Office.

Recreating the Console Program as a GUI

Create a new project by clicking the *Project...* link next to *Create:*, or by clicking the *File* menu, then *New*, then *Project*. The *New Project* screen allows you to specify many different options for the new project. There are several *project templates* for each of the *project types*. The GUI application we create will be a CLR Windows Forms Application project. CLR stands for Common Language Runtime. CLR is the underlying framework provided by Microsoft in which all .Net applications run. To create a CLR Windows Form Application project, follow these steps (and refer to Figure 41):

1. Choose *CLR* under *Project Types*.
2. Choose *Windows Forms Application* under *Templates*.

FIGURE 41 Create a New Windows Forms Application Project

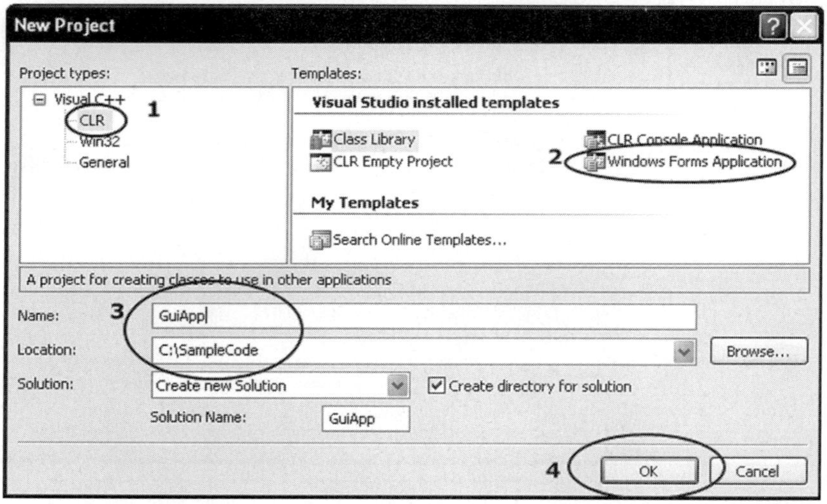

3. Provide a name for the project in the *Name* text field.
4. Click the *OK* button.

   The IDE will look slightly different for the GUI application than it did for the console application (see Figure 42). In the *Workspace* area, there will be a *Form Designer*, which is used to visually design a form (also known as screen) for your GUI application. There will also be a Solution Explorer available to the left and a Toolbox window to the right.

5. If you do not see your Toolbox window, it may be collapsed. Check the right side of the IDE and if you see a small area called "Toolbox", just hover your mouse over the toolbox title.

FIGURE 42 C++.Net IDE for Windows Forms Applications

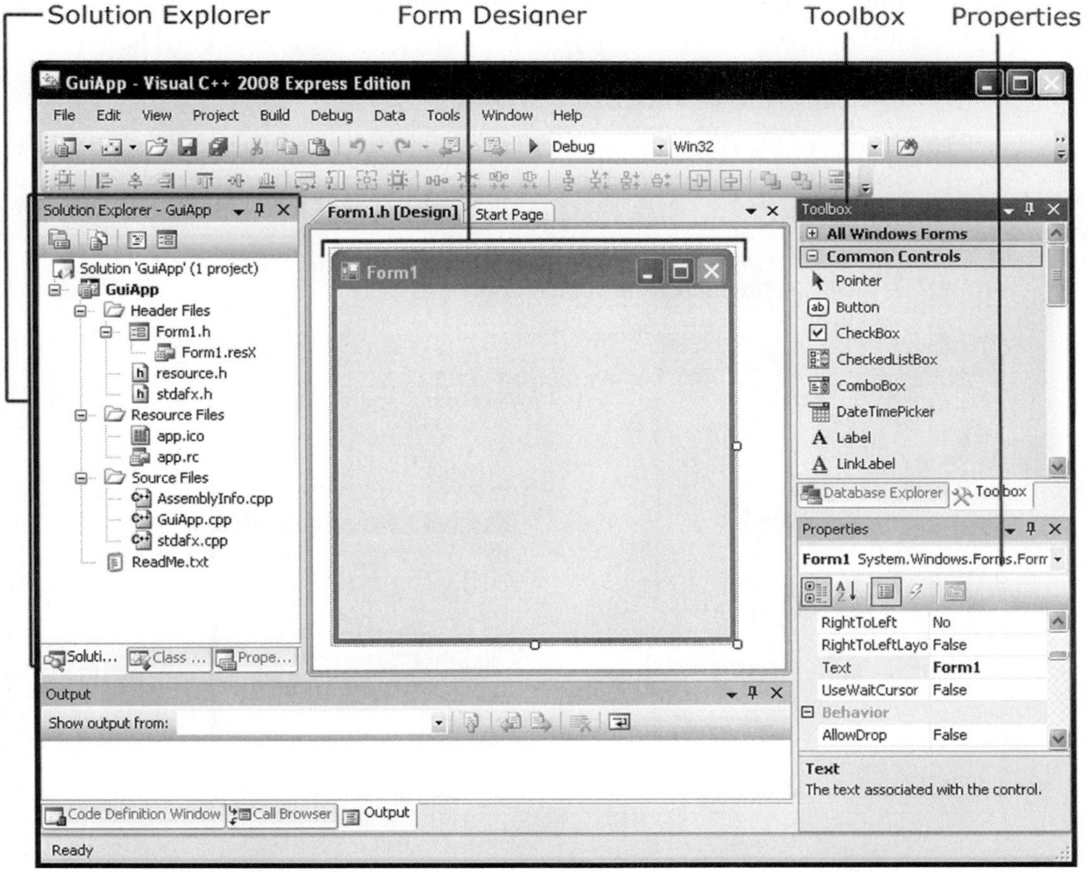

6. Make sure to expand the *Common Controls* area of the *Toolbox* by clicking the plus sign next to *Common Controls*. You can click the small *Pin* icon to keep the toolbox window open at all times (this is recommended).

7. A helpful window to always have open is the *Properties* window. If you do not see a *Properties* window, click the *View* menu, then *Other Windows*, then *Properties Window*. You may also choose to click the small *Pin* icon on the *Properties Window* to keep it open at all times (this is recommended).

8. Click and drag the following controls from the Toolbox onto the Form Designer:
   a. 2 *Label* controls
   b. 2 *TextBox* controls
   c. 1 *Button* control

9. Customize the *Label* controls so that the first one reads "Fahrenheit" and the second one reads "Celsius". (See Figure 43 for details)
   a. Click the control
   b. Click the *Properties Window*
   c. Change the *Text Property* and hit the *Enter* key.

10. Return to the *Form Designer* and click the *Button* control. Now click on the *Properties* window and change the *Text* property to *Convert*.

FIGURE 43 Changing Text Property on a Label Control

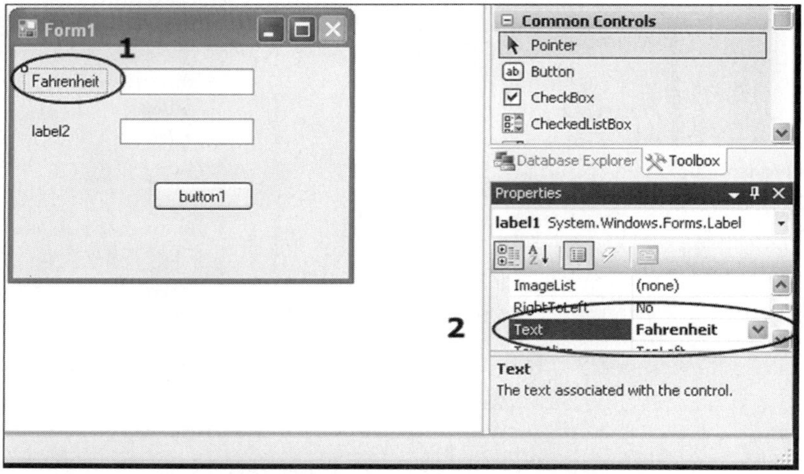

Graphical User Interface (GUI) Applications

```
System::Double dblFahrenheit;
System::Double dblCelsius;

dblFahrenheit = System::Double::Parse(textBox1->Text);
dblCelsius = (dblFahrenheit-32) / 1.8;

System::String^ strDisplay = dblCelsius.ToString();
textBox2->Text = strDisplay;
```

11. Double-click on the *Button* control with the left mouse button. This will open the code window. Type the following code into the already defined `System::Void button1_Click()` function. Figure 44 shows what the completed function should look like.
12. The form should look something like the sample in Figure 45.
13. Hit F5 to run and test the program.

FIGURE 44 Completed Code for `button1_Click()`

```
private: System::Void button1_Click(System::Object^  sender, System::EventArgs^  e)
         {
             System::Double dblFahrenheit;
             System::Double dblCelsius;

             dblFahrenheit = System::Double::Parse(textBox1->Text);
             dblCelsius = (dblFahrenheit-32) / 1.8;

             System::String^ strDisplay = dblCelsius.ToString();
             textBox2->Text = strDisplay;
         }
```

FIGURE 45 Completed Form Design

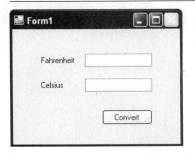

Week Number Finder GUI Project

The .Net CLR provides many features that are already built and ready for you to take advantage of in your own applications. A few good examples are all the pre-built UI controls such as the label, textbox and button previously demonstrated in the Temperature Converter GUI application. The next set of steps will guide you through creating a Week Number Finder application which will make use of the convenient *MonthCalendar* control. The end result will look similar to the application shown in Figure 46.

Create a new CLR GUI application as before (refer to Figure 41 if needed) so you have a new blank form as shown in Figure 42, and then perform the following steps:

1. Click and drag the following controls from the *Toolbox* onto the Form Designer (see *Toolbox* icons to the right):
   a. 1 *MonthCalendar* control
   b. 1 *Label* control
   c. 1 *Button* control
2. Change the property values of each control shown in the table below. Refer to Figure 43 for guidance on changing a property value for a control.

Control	Property Name	Property Value
Label	Name	lblWeekNumber
Label	Text	Week #
Button	Name	btnShowWeekNumber
Button	Text	Show Week #

FIGURE 46 Week # Finder Form Design

3. Double-click on the *Button* control with the left mouse button. This will open the code window. Type in the code shown below in Figure 47.
4. Scroll to the top of the code window where you see several "using namespace" lines and add the following line of code.

```
using namespace System::Globalization;
```

5. Save all your work (refer to Figure 25 for the Save All option in the File menu).
6. Hit F5 to run and test the program. If you are prompted that your project is out of date, click the `Yes` button to build the latest code updates you made.
7. In the running application, click any day of the week and then click the `Show Week #` button. You should see the week number label update based on the day you currently have selected in the *MonthCalendar* control.

FIGURE 47 Week Finder Application Code

```
private: System::Void btnShowWeekNumber_Click( System::Object^ sender,
                                                System::EventArgs^ e)
         {
                Int32 weekNum = GetWeekNumber(monthCalendar1->SelectionStart);
                String^ weekNumString = weekNum.ToString();
                lblWeekNumber->Text = "Week #" + weekNumString;
         }
private: System::Int32 GetWeekNumber( System::DateTime dtPassed )
         {
                Calendar^ cal = CultureInfo::CurrentCulture->Calendar;
                Int32 weekNum = cal->GetWeekOfYear( dtPassed,
                                        CalendarWeekRule::FirstFourDayWeek,
                                        DayOfWeek::Sunday );
                return weekNum;
         }
```

Index

A
Add Watch button, 26
Applications. *See also* Programs; Projects
   CLR Windows Forms Application, 28–33
   described, 5
   Win 32 Application Wizard, 13–17
AutoHide, 12

B
Breakpoints
   defined, 19
   setting, 20–22
   using, 20
Build menu, 16
Build Solution, 16
Building programs, 16
Button control, 30, 31

C
Closing IDE windows, 12
CLR (Common Language Runtime), 28
CLR Windows Forms Application project, 28–31
Code stepping
   defined, 19
   exercise in, 23–24
   keyboard shortcuts, 23
   setting next execution step, 25–26
   Step Into, 22
   Step Out, 23
   Step Over, 22
Collapsing IDE windows, 12
Common Controls, 30

Console program
   creating, 13–18
   recreating as GUI, 28–31
Cursor, 3

D
Debugging
   breakpoints, 19, 20–22
   code stepping exercise, 23–24
   Debug menu, 17, 20, 21, 22, 23
   Debug toolbar, 22, 23
   defined, 19
   keyboard shortcut for, 17, 20, 21
   running with and without, 17
   setting next execution step, 25–26
   stepping through code, 19, 21–23
   watching variables, 20
Disk space for installation, 8–10
Disks and files/folders, 3–5
Docking IDE windows, 11–12

E
Error messages, 16–17

F
File menu, 18, 28
Files
   ConsoleApp.cpp, 15
   folders and, 3–5
Floppy drive, 5
Form Designer, 29–31

G
Getting Started, 13
Graphical IDE, installing, 8–9

Graphical User Interface (GUI)
    CLR Windows Forms Application project, 28–31
    overview, 28
    recreating Console program as, 28–31

H

Hidden IDE windows, 12

I

Icons, desktop, 3
IDE (Integrated Development Environment)
    menus, 12
    starting, 11
    toolbars, 12
    working with windows in, 11–12
    workspace, 12, 15
Insert Breakpoint, 20
Installing software
    Destination Folder, 9, 10
    Download and Install Progress window, 10–11
    downloading setup program, 5–7
    Internet connection requirement, 10
    MSDN Library option, 8
    registration, 11
    Visual C++ 2008 Express Edition, 5–11

K

Keyboard shortcuts
    Code Stepping, 22–23
    Debug Start, 19
    Start debugging, 19
    Start Without Debugging, 17

L

Label control, 30
Local Disk (C:), 3

M

Menus
    Build menu, 16
    Debug menu, 17, 20, 21, 22, 23
    File menu, 18, 28
    in IDE, 12
Microsoft Windows. *See* Windows (Microsoft)
MSDN Library installation, 8
My Computer, 3, 4

N

New Project screen, 13

O

Opening existing projects, 18–19
Operating system. *See* Windows (Microsoft)
Options, installing, 8–9
Output window, 15, 16

P

Password, login, 2
Pin icon, 30
Precompiled header, 14
Programs
    building, 16
    creating Console program, 13–18
    customizing skeleton, 15

recreating Console program as GUI, 28–31
running, 17
Projects
    CLR Windows Forms Application project, 28–31
    opening existing, 18–19
    saving, 18
    starting new, 13, 28
    templates, 13, 28
    Win 32 Application Wizard, 12–13
Properties window, 30
Pushpin icon and AutoHide, 12

Q
Quick Watch, 26–27

R
Recent Projects list, 13
Running programs, 17–18

S
Saving projects, 18
Skeleton program, 15–17
Solution Explorer, 15, 29
Start Button, 2
Start Page, 13, 18
Stepping through code. *See* Code stepping
System Tray, 2

T
Task Bar, 2
Templates for projects, 13, 28
TextBox control, 30

Toolbars
    Debug, 22–25
    IDE, 12
Toolbox window, 29–30

U
User name, login, 1–2

V
Variables, watching, 20
Visual C++ 2008 Express Edition
    IDE. *See* IDE (Integrated Development Environment)
    installing, 5–11
    overview, 5
    registering, 11

W
Watch
    Add Watch button, 26
    Quick Watch, 26–27
    on variables, defined, 20
Win 32 Application Wizard, 13–17
Window Tabs, 12
Windows (IDE), working with, 12
Windows (Microsoft)
    defined, 1
    desktop, 2–3
    logging in, 1–2
    My Computer, 3, 4
    navigating the environment, 1–5
    Windows 2000, 1, 2, 3
    Windows XP, 1, 2, 3
Windows Forms Application Project, 28–31

Wizard, Win 32 Application, 13–17
Workspace
 defined, 12
 Form Designer, 29–31
 open file in, 15
 setting breakpoints, 20–22
 Start Page, 13, 18

Notes

Notes

Notes

Notes

Notes